Spiritual Opposition

TO THE 5-FOLD MINISTRY

H. A. Lewis

ISBN: Soft cover   978-0-9904360-2-7

This book was printed in the United States of America.

PROLOGUE

This teaching was given to me after eight months of prayer and fasting. God gave me revelation of the spiritual opposition to each office of the five-fold ministry. My prayer is that you receive the knowledge this book holds so you will surround yourself in prayer and in the word of God as you walk out your calling and not take it lightly.

We are in a spiritual warfare against the world, the flesh and the devil. His agenda is to come against you in any way he can.

DEDICATION

This book is dedicated to my precious wife, Patricia. She has been my most loyal friend and the one who makes the book come to life. Thank you for all your hard work.

OPPOSITION TO THE FIVE FOLD MINISTRY

Satan	Absolute ruler and prince of darkness; god of this world; destroyer; adversary of God and humankind; personal name of the devil
Principalities	Rulers under Satan; establish legalism and bondage; stand against God's law and nature; blockers of God's message; can rule over a region
Spiritual Wickedness	Perverted instructors; teach witchcraft and false religion; organization of devilish spirits that work evil and mischief for the purpose of humanity's deception and destruction
Rulers of Darkness	Perverted shepherds; steals Word, leads to strange pastures; delegates influences of control; high ranking evil, false gods of the world's nations
Powers	Force of dark power; power to perform activities or deeds but no authority; spread spiritual darkness and blindness; cause sickness and death; brings into slavery of false gods and goddesses

TABLE of CONTENTS

Introduction:

Understanding the Five Fold Ministries and Their Spiritual Opposition

1

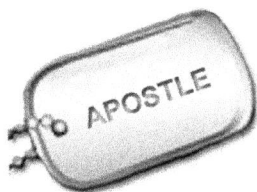

THE APOSTLE

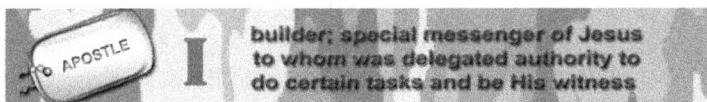

APOSTLE

builder; special messenger of Jesus
to whom was delegated authority to
do certain tasks and be His witness

THE APOSTLE

Apostle: One who is sent by God to establish local assemblies and to appoint pastors, teachers, evangelists, and prophets. He is like the Heart revealing compassion & strategy for advancing the Kingdom.

Ephesians 4:11 – *And He gave some apostles*
We have now come to the last position of the fivefold ministry. It is the absolute highest level of the governmental structure of God's kingdom on Earth.

As we have seen, the teacher is opposed by spiritual wickedness in high places, the evangelist by rulers of darkness of this world, pastors by the powers that be, prophets by the principalities, but there seems to be no opposing force against the apostle.

Ephesians 6:12 seems to mention no hindrance to the ministry of the apostle, but this is not true because the great apostle Paul states that Satan himself has buffeted Paul on all sides, and that he personally had hindered Paul from coming to the people.

Just as God gave permission to the adversary to put Job to the test, it seems that God allows the enemy to test the character of the apostle.

Today belief in five fold ministry is rare. The office of the apostle is thought to simply be that of the missionary. Yes, it is true that the missionary is sent out by their denomination to establish churches and church schools in areas where there are no works.

Yes, Paul and Silas were set aside and sent out to establish works for God's kingdom. In every sense of the word they were missionaries. But, they were more than that. They were called by God to be apostles.

It is almost impossible to separate the apostle and the missionary since their job description seems to be identical. But the apostle is the office God chose to be over the fivefold ministry. Yes, the apostle will seem to act like a missionary going into areas where there are no churches.

Once he starts a fellowship, he will stay with the newly established fellowship until it is able to establish their own local church government, prophet, pastor, evangelist, and teachers. After seeing that they are in good hands and things are going according to God's design, he then is free to move on to new territories to start all over again. If you study the life of Paul you will see that he was always on the move. If he was not in prison, he was building new works, or revisiting older churches he had started. When he was not doing this he was training young pastors as in the care of Timothy and Titus.

He was also busy defending the faith and writing letters of instruction and encouragement, as well as correction to the churches.

You see the apostle John doing the same in his epistles, as well as in the book of **(Revelation in Chapter1&2)**. Peter, as well as James, does the same thing. These epistles are books of instructions to help the believers to go on in maturity. The apostles labor to increase the kingdom of God on Earth, and to make sure that God's Word is correctly taught.

The life of the apostle can be a very difficult one, but highly rewarding Paul writes in **(2 Corinthians 4:8-10)**.

We are troubled on every side, yet not distressed; We are perplexed but not in despair; persecuted but not forsaken; cast down but not destroyed. Always bearing about in the body the dying of the Lord Jesus, that the life also of Jesus might be made manifest in our body.

With the office of the apostle comes great responsibility. **It is not an office which anyone should try to take upon themselves.**

Looking at the testimony of what Paul endured for the sake of the Gospel, should make one cautious about taking a title that God did not give them for themselves.

Just listen to what Paul says in (2 Corinthians 11:17-30).

Paul begins with

That which I speak, I speak not after the Lord, but as it were foolishly, in this confidence of boasting. Seeing that many glory after the flesh, I will glory also. For ye suffer fools gladly, seeing ye yourselves are wise. For ye suffer, if a man brings you into bondage. If a man devour you, if a man take of you, if a man exalt himself, if a man smite you on the face. I speak as concerning reproach, as through we had been weak. How be it where in so ever any is bold, I speak foolishly, I am bold also. Are there any Hebrews? So am I. Are they the seed of Abraham? So am I. Are they ministers of Christ? I speak as a fool. I am more; In labor more abundant, in stripes above measure, In prison more frequent, in death oft. Of the Jews five times received I forty stripes save one. Thrice was I beaten with rods, once was I stoned, thrice I suffered shipwreck, a night and day I have been in the deep; In journeying often, in perils of water, in perils of robbers; in perils by my own countrymen, in perils by the heathens, in perils of the city, in perils of the wilderness, in perils in the sea, in perils among false brethrens; In weariness and painfulness, in watching often, in hunger and thirst, in fasting often, in cold and nakedness. Beside those things that are without, that which comes upon me daily the care of all the churches. Who is weak, and I am not weak? Who is offended, and I burn not? If I must needs glory, I will glory of the things which concerns my infirmities.

To read that this great man of God endured for the sake of the Gospel and because of his position in the five fold ministry should make us all very cautious about taking titles to ourselves.

So far we have found that the teacher faces spiritual wickedness in high places. The evangelist faces the darkness of this world. The pastor faces the powers that be. The prophet faces principalities, as in the case of Elijah and the prophets of Baal, but what does the apostle face?

In **(Ephesians 6:12)** it states that *we wrestle not against flesh and blood, but against principalities, against powers, against the rulers of darkness of this world and against spiritual wickedness in high places.* These are all terrible and powerful foes that can wreak havoc wherever they are.

Also they can team up together to come against any of God's people, especially those in governmental positions. We know the enemy of the teacher, the evangelist, the pastor, and the prophet, but what about the apostle of God. Who opposes him?

I believe that all **four of the opponents** we have studied so far will join together to come against him. Yet there is one more enemy that is far worse than those four and the answer is found in

(1 Thessalonians 2:18). It reads, *Wherefore we would have come unto you, even I Paul, once and again but Satan hinders me.*

2

SPIRITUAL OPPOSITION TO THE APOSTLE
Satan (Job 1:6; Revelation 12:9)

destroyer; great opposer or adversary of God and humankind; the personal name of the devil

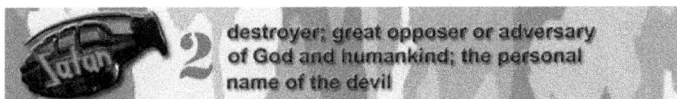

SPIRITUAL OPPOSITION TO THE APOSTLE
Satan (Job 1:6; Revelation 12:9)

1. Satan – Adversary, the accuser, the thief, the liar, and murderer.

2. Lucifer – Deceiving angel of light, son of the morning, king of Tyrus - (**Ezekiel 28:12-19**)

3. The anointed cherub that covereth.

4. The prince of the world. (**John 12:31, John 16:11**)

5. Roaring lion (**1 Peter 5:8**)

6. Wicked one (**John 10:10**)

7. Belial (**2 Corinthians 6:15**)

8. Beelzebub - Prince of devils (**Matthew 10:25, 12:24**)

9. Corrupter of the minds (**2 Corinthians 11:3**)

10. Oppressor (**Acts 10:38**)

11. Red dragon, Serpent (**Revelation 12:3, 20:2-7; 2 Corinthians 11:3, Genesis 3:1, 14, Revelation 12:9**)

12. God of this world (**2 Corinthians 4:4**)

Yes, the opponent to the apostle of God is the devil himself. It is like any army on the Earth, you do not send a private to face a general in battle, and a general does not surrender to anyone below his military rank.

He surrenders to someone his equal or higher. Just like the betrayal of Jesus, the enemy did not trust it to any of his rank or file; instead, he took it upon himself to enter into Judas (**John 13:27**) to see that it was done properly.

You see the adversary tempting Jesus in the desert, you see him hindering the great apostle Paul. Peter warns us to be careful for your adversary goes about as a roaring lion to seek and destroy.

The devil or Satan as he is called is very much alive and active in (**Job chapters 1 & 2**). You see him debating with God over the life of Job. In the book of **Genesis**, he deceived Eve and in the book of Jude he argues with Michael the great arch angel and defender of Israel over the body of Moses. In (**Revelation 2:10**) we see the devil causing the saints to be thrown into prison.

Satan is a murderer, a liar, and a thief who comes to kill, steal, and destroy, and he will use all that he has to come against God's apostles. He will do everything in his powers to hinder the work of the apostle and to stop the growth of God's kingdom on the Earth.

Now you may feel that you are safe because God has not called you to any of these positions, but you are a believer and you have an enemy. His name is Satan and he has an army which he uses against God's people. We must all stay under the blood and remain filled with the Spirit. We are in a war that will not end until the Lord comes and finally defeats the adversary and his allies.

Put on the whole armor of God, that you may be able to stand against the wiles of the devil.

Stay fully dressed in the Lord's armor, stay filled with the Spirit and the Word, pray one for another and proclaim loudly and proudly the name of Jesus Christ, and watch as every knee must bow and every tongue confess that he is Lord, to the glory of God the Father. Ephesians 6:10-18

The Lord bless you and keep you safe. Amen!

And he gave some, apostles; and some,
prophets; and some, evangelists; and some,
pastors and teachers
Ephesians 4:11 (KJV)

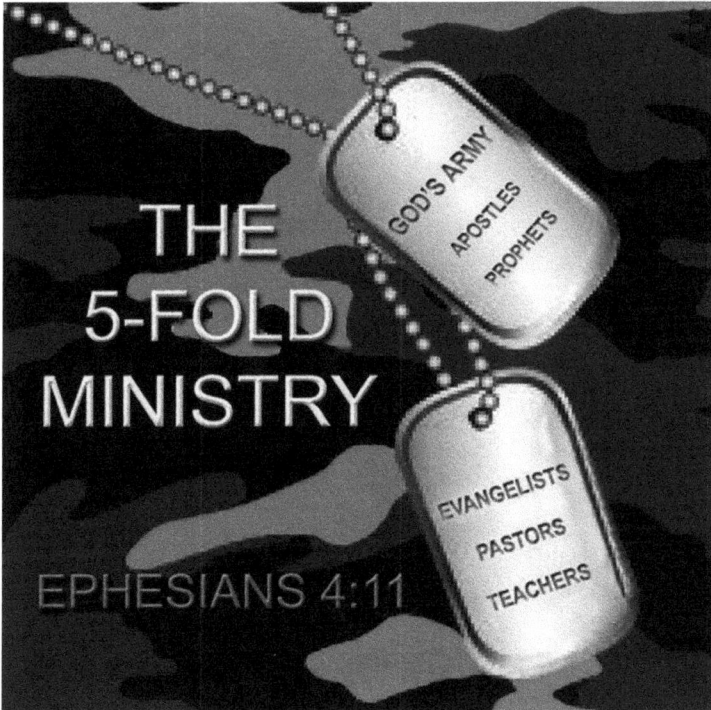

THE 5-FOLD MINISTRY

EPHESIANS 4:11

GOD'S ARMY
APOSTLES
PROPHETS
EVANGELISTS
PASTORS
TEACHERS

3

THE PROPHET

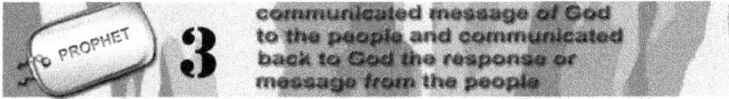

3 communicated message of God to the people and communicated back to God the response or message from the people

THE PROPHET

Prophet – A spokesmen for God. One who speaks to God on the behalf of man and to man on the behalf of God bringing a word of encouragement and chastisement.

One who speaks to God concerning men, the church, the nations and their rulers. He is the like the mouth communicating guidance.

Malachi 4:5 *Behold I will send you Elijah, the prophet, before the coming of the great and dreadful day of the Lord.*

The office of the prophet is the most sought after position of the five fold ministry. Yet it is also the most misunderstood. Most people, who are used in the gift of prophecy, automatically feel that they are prophets. This is not true. The gift of prophecy is given to an individual at a time when the Holy Spirit deems it necessary. Even a babe in Christ can be used in the gift. You do not need to be mature in order to be used.

Please keep in mind that God used a donkey to confront Balaam in the Old Testament. God will use whatsoever He will to deliver his message at the time he chooses to do so.

The gift of prophecy is an awesome gift. Paul stated that we should all seek to prophesy. As wonderful as this gift is, it is not the office of the prophet.

The prophets in the Old Testament were amazing men of God. We all delighted in the story of Elijah facing the false prophets of Baal and how God answered his prayer by fire.

We read in awe how Moses held his staff high as God parted the red sea. There prophets had amazing abilities.

They could call down fire from heaven. They could hold back the rain so it would not rain upon the Earth until they called for it. All of this was phenomenal, but it was not the major calling in their life. Their main purpose was to speak to the nation of Israel on the behalf of God. To warn them of their sinful ways, to bring Israel back to a right standing with Adonai, the Lord their God.

On a more serious note, these amazing prophets of God had their weaknesses. Moses complained of being slow of speech. Elijah had the courage to face the four hundred prophets of Baal, but ran from a woman Jezebel. Jonah was prejudice and ran from the call to go to Nineveh, because he knew God was merciful and would forgive the nation of Nineveh if they repented.

With all their weaknesses and all their strengths, they were still used mightily by God. Daniel was used to prophesy to five different Kings from Nebuchadnezzar to Cyrus.

Joseph prophesied to his family and then to Pharaoh. The Minor Prophets spoke of prophecy that would come to past hundreds of years in the future. Zechariah spoke as clearly of the last days as did Daniel.

Ezekiel spoke of the armies of Gog and Magog, and the Kings of the North who came against Israel in the final days.

All of these prophets who were called by God to fill the office paid with their lives. They were burnt to death, stoned, fed to the lions, sewn into animal skins and then feed to wild beasts. Others were placed in logs and cut in half.

These great prophets of old had great and powerful enemies. Some included humans, Pharaoh who claimed to be a god, Jezebel a daughter of a priest of Bel, and even a Caesar who established improper worship. All were motivated by unseen principalities who hated them and the god they served.

It is no different today, the principalities that have exalted themselves and have opposed the kingdom of God, are still in position to come against the New Testament prophets.

Our battle is not with flesh or blood, but against the principalities, against the powers, against the world rulers of darkness, against the spiritual hosts of wickedness in heavenly places. **Ephesians 6:12**

4

SPIRITUAL OPPOSITION TO THE PROPHET

PRINCIPALITIES

blockers of God's message; a powerful
ruler, any type of rule other than the
rule of God himself over a region

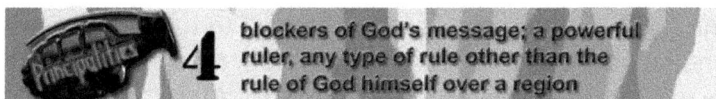

SPIRITUAL OPPOSITION TO THE PROPHET
Principalities

Please note that our battle is not with flesh or blood, but against the principalities, against the powers, against the world rulers of darkness, against the spiritual hosts of wickedness in heavenly places.

Principalities – The concept of principalities is understood by the Greek word "Arche" meaning chief of rulers. These principalities are ruling spirits possessing executive authority or governmental rule in the world.

These ruling spirits are usually over nations, cities, towns, villages, churches, families and even individuals.

American Heritage Dictionary defines principalities as:
1.) Territory ruled by a prince or from which a prince obtains his title. (**Daniel 10**)

When Satan rebelled against God, he was thrown out of heaven. The Bible states in the book of Revelation that when the great red dragon was defeated by Michael, he took one third of the stars with him. (**Revelation 12:4**) These stars were symbolic of the angels. Simply put one third of God's angels chose to follow Satan in his rebellion.

They were cast out of the third heaven where God's throne is and lodged in the second heaven where Satan established his throne and the fallen angels became the principalities of the air.

Satan, or the Adversary as he is referred to in Hebrew, is the unchallenged leader of this group of fallen angels called the sons of God in **(Genesis 6:2), (Job 1:6), (Job 2:1)**. Even those who rebelled against the Lord are still called the sons of God, because like mankind he created them.

On the Day of Judgment they will stand before the Lord and will reap their just punishment. For now, they are under the leadership of the god of this world, the prince of darkness. They are given territories to rule over. They guard their area very well, whether it is a country, a town or a church, or even a family.

They use all of their diabolical intelligence to lead as many as they can astray by false religions, the occult, humanism, evolution, and by pride.

In the Old Testament, God gave strict orders to the nation of Israel to not follow the ways of the pagan gentile nations around them. When Israel obeyed God, Jehovah blessed them mightily. When they went after the ways of the nations around them, served other gods and intermarried with the heathen, God sent prophets to warn them of their errors to turn them back to righteousness. But, many times, the influence of these false gods, and their ways were so strong that instead of obeying the word of the Lord, and listening to His prophets' warning(s), the Israelites ignored God's warnings and destroyed them.

Many rose up against God's prophets and destroyed them. False self-appointed prophets, who were prophesying prosperity, blessings and material gain, during the same time, as when the Word of Jehovah proclaimed judgment, resisted prophets like Isaiah, Jeremiah, and Ezekiel. You can see how strongly God's prophets were resisted and attacked by the principalities that were over the nations.

If you look carefully at the story of Elijah the prophet who God loved so much he sent down a fiery chariot to bring home to glory. **(1Kings 18:22-40)**

You can also see how hard the false gods fought against Elijah to destroy him and to keep the nation of Israel in bondage to a lie. After Elijah defeated the four hundred and fifty false prophets of Baal, Jezebel, who was the daughter of Ethbaal the king of Zidonians, threatened him.

Jezebel was a devoted worshipper of the false god Baal. Her husband was a very weak willed man who let her control him and make the decisions instead of himself.

You could say that Jezebel was actually one of the first woman libbers in history. The history of Ahab and Jezebel was so wicked they were completely under the control of these powerful principalities that the Lord proclaimed a curse over them. In **(1 Kings 21:23-24)** God stated that dogs at the wall of **Jezreel** would eat Jezebel and that Ahab's descendant who died the city the dogs would eat, and those who died in the fields, the birds of the air would eat.

People think that these principalities and the false prophets they use are no longer in existence today. That is not true! The people may have perished and gone to their judgments, but the principalities are still alive and well on the planet Earth today.

They still use self-appointed prophets and un knowledgeable preachers to preach false doctrines of prosperity today. They preach that God is not angry with America. They say that God is not bringing judgment on us.

They say it is okay that we take the life of the unborn, and

that we must embrace the false religions of this world as in

Islam and Witchcraft.

They teach that same sex marriage is alright, and that
marriage should be done away with.

We are worst today than Sodom and Gomorrah ever was; if
you doubt this, than just take a look at *Ashville, NC, Salem
MA, and Provincetown MA*. All you will see is the occult
and homosexuality and the hatred of God's Word.

Isn't it funny that the gays are getting protection under the
hate law, that witches have right to sell their religious articles
and their philosophies anywhere, and the Muslims can build
their mosque right here in America. Every way of life is
protected by laws <u>except</u> for one; <u>and that is Christianity</u>.

A young Wicca can try to recruit your child in school. They
can carry their material with them without fear of the law.
School teachers can teach your sons and daughters that
homosexuality is just another lifestyle. They can counsel
your teenage daughter to have an abortion without telling
you because it is a woman's right to choose.

All of this is protected by law, but let your child carry a
Bible to school and to share their faith with others, and see
how fast they will be expelled.

Preachers in Arizona, California, and even in Texas have
already been arrested for having Bible studies in their own
home. Just recently in the state of Arizona, a preacher was
arrested and placed in jail for sixty days, and given a $12,000
fine, along with a 3 year probation because his crime was
having a Bible study in his home. Eighteen (18) fully armed
officers of the law stormed into his home as if he were a

homeland terrorist. The reasoning they gave was that the area was not zoned to be a church.

You cannot have a Bible study in your home, but you neighbors can throw a wild pool party, blast the music loudly, while people get drunk and cause all sorts of chaos, but that is okay as long as there are no Bible studies going on.

Tell me that these principalities are not at work today when the president can stand up publicly and declare we are no longer a Christian nation, but we are a nation of many gods and religions, and no one protests.

Or when three public servants, one being the President proclaims as Israel did in their arrogance that, *the bricks are fallen down, but we will rebuild with hewn stones; the sycamores are cut down, but we will change them into cedars* **(Isaiah 9:10)**. This is not a blessing but an arrogant reply to God's judgment of Israel, and still holds as an arrogant reply to God's judgment towards America.

For those of you who believe you are prophets, please be aware that principalities will oppose you at every hand.

We need to stay in close relationship with the Lord, and stay under His blood and His covering.

Understand you cannot fight these principalities without the Lord's help, guidance and even timing.

Many have tried to stand on their own strength and their own knowledge with the result being that they have fallen.

Remember prophets, the battle is not yours, but the Lord's, and it is not by power or might, but by God's Spirit that we win. (Zech 4:6)

The book of Revelation states that they overcome him (Satan) by the Word of their testimony, and the blood of the Lamb, and they loved not their life unto the death. **(Rev 12:11)**

A prophet has a great calling.

You have been chosen to speak to man on the behalf of God, to give warning to the church when it is drifting away from God, as in **(Revelation;(Chapters 1 & 2)**. You are also called to speak to God on the behalf of man. Take your calling seriously because in these days of unrighteousness it may cost you your life. Pray much and consume God's Word.

Do not rely on anyone else to teach you. *Instead study to show yourself approved unto God, a workman that needeth not to be ashamed, rightly dividing the word of truth.* **(2 Timothy 2:15)**

May God watch over you and protect you, keep you as you stand in the gap for His people. Keep in mind that the office of the prophet is a lonely one. You will not have many friends, and the religious people will hate and despise you, for you will be a thorn in their side, as they play their religious games. Yet, your rewards will be great if you remain faithful and do not compromise. God Bless!

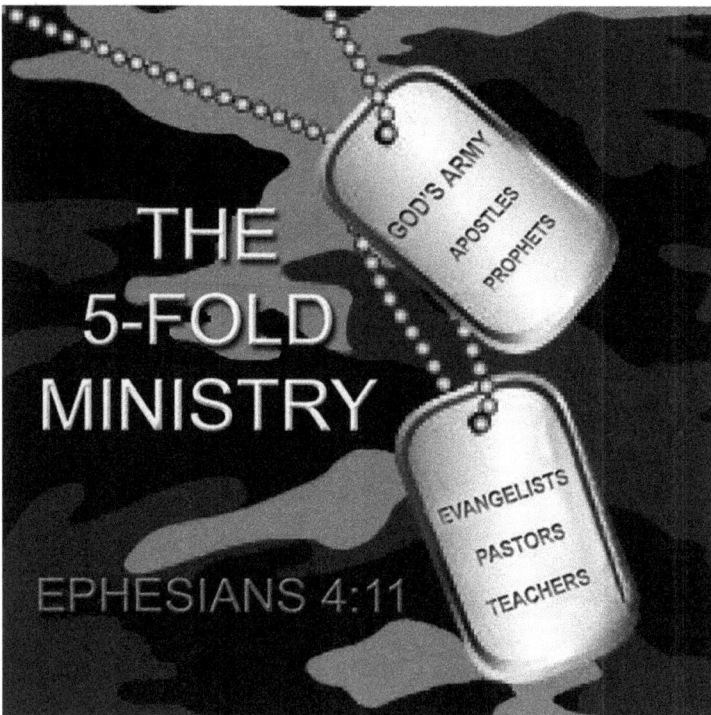

THE 5-FOLD MINISTRY

GOD'S ARMY
APOSTLES
PROPHETS

EVANGELISTS
PASTORS
TEACHERS

EPHESIANS 4:11

5

THE EVANGELIST

gatherer, breaks chains of bondage; one who proclaims good tidings that is not attached to a particular church, takes good tidings where Spirit leads

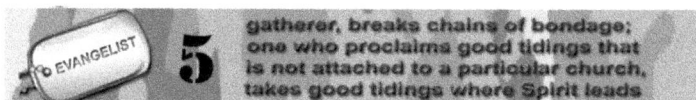

THE EVANGELIST

Evangelist: the preacher of the Gospel, spreader of good news, revivalist, bringing people to repentance, and conviction. These are the hands that are always reaching out to souls.

A voice in the desert cried out repent for the kingdom of God draweth near. (John the Baptist, (**Mark 1:15**)

This is an interesting quote concerning the evangelist by C.S. Lewis. Mr. Lewis stated where a speaker has that gift; the direct evangelical appeal of "come to Jesus" type can be as over-whelming today as it was a hundred years ago. Lewis stated, "I cannot do it, but those who can, ought to do it with all their might." Lewis goes on to say that I am not sure that the ideal missionary team ought not to consist of one who argues and one who (in the fullest sense of the word) preaches. Put up your arguer first to undermine the intellectual prejudice; then let the evangelist proper launch his appeal.

Evangelist: yours is a great responsibility. You are not the shepherd of the flock whose responsibility is to feed and water, and care for the sheep. Please do not be offended by this statement. Always remember every allegories limit. You, evangelist, are like the sheep dog with all of its glory. It is their job to help the shepherd in watching over the sheep. It is their duty to protect the sheep from all enemies from without and to bring back the stray and the lost.

I would watch my dog, who is an Australian Shepherd, when she would cut off or stop my grandson when he was going too far in the yard, or getting too close to the road and danger. She would faithfully cut him off and begin to herd him back to where she felt he was safest.

I have grown spiritually by being under the tutorship and preaching of great men and women of God, who were filled not only with the energy and power of the Holy Spirit, but also deeply knowledgeable in the Word.

I have had the privilege of being friends with R.W. Schambach, Lester Sumrall Derek Prince, Frank Harmon, David Wilkerson who was my wife's spiritual father, as well as the amazing Dr. Leonard W. Hero (former president and pastor of Zion Bible Institute and Zion Gospel Temple)

I remember my wife and I would wait each day for the "**hour of power program" so we could** hear Brother **Schambach**'s sermon and then to hear his signature statement, **"You don't have any problems. All you need is faith in God."**

Yes, it is the oriented words from scripture coming from the mouth of the evangelist, which steers the wayward soul to return to the flock of the Great Shepherd. It is the evangelist that makes the sinner aware that they are in great darkness, and the word preaches by faith coming from the anointed evangelist, all shining forth the eternal light of glory into the realm of darkness setting the captive free.

Remember evangelist; it was God who chose you to do His will. It was not the opposite. Hear what the Lord said through the prophet (**Isaiah in Chapter 43:22-23**), *"But this is a people robbed and spoiled; they are all of the snared in holes, and are hid in prison houses: They are for a prey, and none delivereth: for a spoil and none said restore."*

(**Isaiah 43:23**) *Who among you will give ear to this? Who will hear and hear for the time to come?*

This, evangelist: is why God called you not to build a kingdom for self but to extend the kingdom of God.

Everywhere your footsteps go God wants to give it to you for the sake of the growth of the kingdom, and the increase of His flock, not yours.

Dear evangelist, like the teacher, you are established to help the pastor. You are an under shepherd of the local church. You fill the church with the anointed power of your evangelical words. The pastor watches closely over each new convert. Each yearling, so to say, is under the teacher, who is under the pastor, who instructs through their anointed teaching until they are healthy and mature. This is the power of unity.

Keep in mind the words of the psalmist, when he stated: Behold, how good and how pleasant it is for the brethren to dwell together in unity!

It is like the precious ointment upon the head, which ran down upon the beard, even Aaron's beard: that went down to the skirts of his garments; As the dew of Her'mon, and as the dew that descended upon the mountain of Zion: for there the Lord commanded the blessing, even life forever more (**Psalms 133**)

Yes, evangelist, yours is a great responsibility. It is given to you, the power to speak life, where there is death, light where there is darkness, freedom where there is bondage, hope where there is hopelessness, joy for sorrow, and accost there will be miracles following your ministry.

Blind eyes will be open, the deaf will hear, the lame will walk, and even the dead will rise, and the greatest of all miracles...souls will be born again. Keep in mind that with all these wonderful blessings, you like the teacher, will also have an enemy to oppose you at every turn.

The teacher is opposed by wicked spirits in high places, and you, oh evangelist, the sharer of truth and light, are in **direct opposition** to the rulers of darkness in this world.

As you stand for truth and share the word of God, which is the bread of Life to the hungry prisoners, the rulers of darkness do all they can to diminish the light that will expose all the deeds of darkness. Please remember, Mr. Or Mrs. Evangelist, if you are not filled with the Word, which is the bread of Life, and with the Spirit of God, which is the living water, then you have nothing to give to those who are hungering and thirsting for righteousness.

Evangelist, remember you are **not** called to build up your own ministry, but rather build up your own kingdom of God. So many today forget that they represent God and the local church. They are sometimes guilty of taking away the finances of the local body. Books, tapes, CDs and DVDs are a good thing, and may even bless those who listen or read them. There is nothing wrong in the evangelist prospering financially, but make sure you are not taking away from the tithes and offering that should be going to the local church.

Do not let the enemy of your soul deceive you into believing that you have no one over you spiritually to answer to. Always remember that you are an extension of the local body of believers. You should have a pastor to whom you submit to; so that the power of darkness which will try to oppose you cannot get a strong hold on you. Many would claim that their ministry of evangelism is world famous and are too busy to report to the local body of believers and to a pastor of a local church.

Always remember that it is God who promotes, expands and gives increase to any ministry, and we are subjective to His rules. If we do not follow His way than pride will set in and pride always comes before the fall.

Keep in mind the words of Lucifer before he fell from his exalted position.

"How art those fallen from heaven, O Lucifer, son of the morning! How art thou cut down to the ground, which did weaken the nation! For thou hast said in thine heart, I will ascend into heaven, I will exalt my throne above the stars of God: I will sit also upon the mount of the congregation, in the side of the North. I will ascend above the heights of the clouds; I will be like the most high **(Isaiah 14:12-14).**

Lucifer was filled with pride and self- importance. He felt that because of his beauty, wisdom and talents, as well as his position, and God was more than able to remove them.

As I have said before, evangelist, yours is a great responsibility. It is by your preaching that you sway men to become believers. It is through the anointing of the Holy Spirit that miracles, signs and wonders accord while you are ministering to those who are oppressed, obsessed and even possessed of unclean spirits.

The evangelist's work of spreading light and truth is attacked on all sides.

The evangelist who stands on the Word of God, for holiness, and righteousness is now considered to be narrow minded, prejudice and out dated. He is accused of living in the past and being in bondage to a book that is obsolete. When he or she tries as hard as they can to win souls they are blocked on all sides.

6

THE OPPOSITION TO THE EVANGELIST

THE RULERS OF DARKNESS OF THIS WORLD

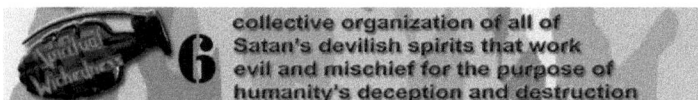

collective organization of all of
Satan's devilish spirits that work
evil and mischief for the purpose of
humanity's deception and destruction

THE OPPOSITION TO THE EVANGELIST
The Rulers Of Darkness Of This World

All who are called to preach the Word of God, and to evangelize to the lost, will find themselves in battle with the ruler of darkness.

They have sat undisturbed and in comfort for generations. They have covered their territory with the darkness of humanism, the occult, homosexuality, and new age philosophy and teachings. They continue to spread false doctrines of Liberalism and the emerging church. They keep the preaching of the blood, the crucifixion, the resurrection, and the return of Christ for His church from being preached.

The doctrine of Hell and Sin has been done away with. In its place is a teaching of a soothing type of love. The doctrine of repentance, revival, holiness, righteousness, and commitment to God and His Word is blocked.

The evangelist's work of spreading light and truth is attacked on all sides. The evangelist who stands on the Word of God, for holiness, and righteousness is now considered to be narrow minded, prejudice and out dated. He is accused of living in the past and being in bondage to a book that is obsolete. When he or she tries as hard as they can to win souls they are blocked on all sides.

He or she may fast or pray. Yet it seems as if their sermon bounces off the ceiling and lands flat on the floor. Why is this happening?

What are the powers working against the evangelist? What keeps the response to his preaching so unsuccessful?

Many good evangelists begin to doubt their call and begin to slow down their ministry, or even stop it altogether.

They never realize that they are under an attack by the rulers of darkness who have been challenged before and will do their best to stop the spread of God's kingdom on Earth. They are not willing to surrender their dark kingdom to the light of the Gospel.

What can the evangelist do then in order to be sure their ministry will prosper and succeed in doing what God has ordained them to do? The answer is found in (**Matthew 12:29**). The Lord stated, *Or else how can one enter into a strong man's house; and spoil his goods, except he first binds the strong man? And then he will be able to enter and spoil his goods*

Yes, the strong man over the area may have been there for generation upon generation. He may seem to be unbeatable. He may boast of his power and display his strengths, but contrary to his own beliefs is not un defeatable. For as scripture states, *"Greater is He that is in me, than he that is in the world"* (**1 John 4:4**).

Remember evangelist, it is your calling to spread the light of the glorious Gospel everywhere in the kingdom of darkness. You can bring it to the very throne of Satan himself. The rulers of darkness may oppose you, and their armies may come against you, but stand strong for the Lord is your covering and your strength, and you have power to bind these spirits in the name of Jesus, and to conquer the land for His glorious name sake.

Charles Finney was a mighty man of God and a tremendous evangelist. Everywhere he went; whole cities would come to the Lord, bars would close, drunks would sober up and get saved.

Wonderful miracles happened in his ministry. Charles Finney said the secret to his success lied in the fact that he prayed, but also he had two faithful prayer warrior fathers, Noah and another man who history has forgotten, but thankfully heaven still remembers. It was through the prayers of these two men who would go before Finney to the city he was to preach in. There they would rent a small flat, and would stay in prayer until Finney arrived. Then they would move to the next city and do the same.

Through the prayers of these men prayer would bind the rulers of darkness over each city Finney would preach in, and Finney could minister in power!

Evangelist: you need a team of prayer warriors to support you in the battle until you can take the city.

The joy of the Lord is your strength and salvation.
(Nehemiah 8:10)

Through Him (Jesus) you can do all things.
(Philippians 4:13)

The Lord shall supply all your needs according to His riches in glory by Christ Jesus.
(Philippians 4:19)

It is through the sermons of the Pastor that causes the sheep to hunger for spiritual food, so that they turn to the Bible for themselves; so that they can obtain knowledge, wisdom and understanding, and so that they can stay strong, so that they can go out and bring more sheep in.

Pastors do not give birth to sheep.
Sheep give birth to sheep but the Pastor many times helps in the delivery of new baby sheep.

7

THE PASTOR

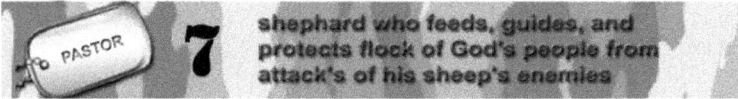

7 shephard who feeds, guides, and protects flock of God's people from attack's of his sheep's enemies

PASTOR

THE PASTOR

Pastor – A minister of the Gospel, related to the Shepherd, Shepherd to the local church.

These are the feet leading the sheep to pasture in the paths of righteousness.

So far we have covered the teacher who is ordained to bring the saints to maturity, and the evangelist is called to shed the light of the Gospel in the darkness of the world. Now we are covering the Pastor, the great under shepherd of the flock of God. It is his job to lead and guide the sheep, to care for the sheep, and to see that they are covered with the oil of the Holy Spirit, the oil of gladness.

He is to stand as David did against the Lion and the bear. In fact, he is to stand against any enemy of the sheep. He must keep in mind these are his father's sheep. Which has been entrusted to him, just as Jesse (the father of David) entrusted his sheep to the care of his son.

It is the Pastor who cares and watches over the flock. He must see that they are lead into green pastures of truth, where they may eat peacefully. He must lead them beside the water of the Holy Spirit, where they may drink freely.

It is through the sermons of the Pastor that causes the sheep to hunger for spiritual food, so that they turn to the Bible for themselves; so that they can obtain knowledge, wisdom and understanding, and so that they can stay strong, so that they can go out and bring more sheep in. Pastors do not give birth to sheep. Sheep give birth to sheep but the Pastor many times helps in the delivery of new baby sheep.

The Pastor's position is of upmost importance. He is the guard of the sheep and their caretaker. If something happens to the Pastor, the sheep are leaderless. The scriptures bear witness to this when it states, Strike the Shepherd and the sheep shall flee. (**Zech 13-7; Mark 14:27**)

Everything that can come against the Pastor will do so. The Pastor needs the support of his people. **He needs a strong wall of prayer around him**. No Pastor, no matter how anointed, or how strong, can stand alone against the powers gathered against them.

There are legions of imps under the control of the strongman over the city and over the local church. They are sent to cause strife and division. They work hard to steal the word before it can take roots in the hearts of the people. They work hard to keep unity from happening in the church. They cause offense to occur in the church. It is their joy to spread discontent, back biting and slander. They are busy creating gossip, defamation of character, accusations, and outright lies. They will do anything to use anyone to destroy the Pastor and his ministry. They will strive to make the Pastor back down and compromise the message.

People need to understand that it is God who appoints leaders, whether they are governmental or spiritual. The elders of the church may feel that they are the ones responsible for the electing of the Pastor. They may feel that the Pastor is accountable to them and that everything he does must be ran by them. This is absolutely wrong!

He is accountable to God. The elders are there to help him, pray for him and give him Godly consult to the Pastor, but they are not there to control him and hinder what God has called him or her to do.

When the Pastor stands before the Lord, he will have to give an account for his life and also for what he or she had done as the under shepherd of the local church. The elders will not have to do this, but they may have to explain why they hindered the Pastor for doing what he was told to do by the Lord.

The Pastor's position is **not** an easy one. Many times they will have to do something the Lord had told them to do. This will cause the Pastor to become unpopular with the secular saints of the local church. Just remember you cannot please all of the people all of the time. You as a Pastor have not been called to please man but instead to please the Lord.

If you will do this then the Lord will add to the church daily those who will be saved. Pastor if you are a praying person, and a word person who is highly favored and anointed of the Lord, you will accomplish great things for the Lord's kingdom.

It will not be easy for there will be great oppression from the power that exalts themselves and opposes the Lord. These powers have been given orders by the enemy of mankind and placed in position to fight you at every turn.

8

THE OPPOSITION TO THE PASTOR:
POWERS OF DARKNESS

ability or strength to perform an activity or deed; having power, but not authority; have physical strength as a lion, bear or wolf

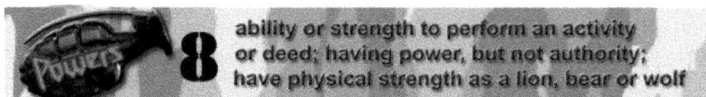

THE OPPOSITION TO THE PASTOR
Powers Of Darkness

The Greek work for power is *exousia*, which means derived or conferred authority, the warrant or rights to do something, or delegated interest or control.

These powers are many times associated with the working of black magic and the fellowshipping with demonic pagan gods, just as worshipping Diana of the Ephesians, Artemis of the Romans, Baal, Moloch, Dragon gods worshipped by the Philistines and the ammonites. (**2 Kings 13:3 KJV**)

In **chapter forty of the book of Job** you find mention of two very power creatures. That seemed to have existed in the day of Job.

One was known as Behemoth and the Lord spoke of the strength of this creature, and further in the next chapter he speaks of the great sea serpent Leviathan. The Lord tells Job that if he ever put his hand forward to battle this creature he would never forget the battle. In (**Psalms 89:9-10**), (**Psalms 87:4**), (**Isaiah 30:7**), (**Ezek 29:2-3**), and (**Job 26:12-13**), we hear of another water creative referred to as **Rahab, the spirit of Egypt**.

The demonic strongman would be enough to cause trouble for any Pastor, but these are just the names of three strongmen who are determined to destroy the Pastor.

TODAY, there is a RETURNING of the ANCIENT SPIRITS of the Old Testament time and some of the Roman and Greek gods and goddesses.

Creatures like Moloch, who the ancient people offered up their children in the fire to him, are alive and well today. People offer up the children, maybe not in the fire as in the old day, but instead they do so through abortion today.

Marduk, the god of Babylon, Chiun, the god of the Philistines, Dragon the fish head god of the Philistines, Diana the goddess of the Ephesians; all which are ancient spirits are returning, and they are standing in opposition to the Pastor.

Pastors cannot even preach against the sins of witchcraft or homosexuality from the pulpit today.

If they do **they will come under the attention of the authorities and be arrested**. There will not even be given a trial. They will just be arrested and placed in jail, just like the brothers in Arizona who were arrested for having Bible studies in their homes.

Church of God, please be warned that there is coming a spiritual darkness to America where the Hollywood style of churches will not be able to stand against the assault that is coming. It will take the fire and power of the Holy Spirit to destroy these powers.

Whole cities in America have come under the diabolical spell of the ancient strongmen of wickedness. If you are wondering why Pastors are burning out and leaving the ministry at the rate of one hundred a day, now you know.

The powers have joined forces to attack your Pastor who may not have a wall of protection around him that a praying church produces.

9

THE TEACHER

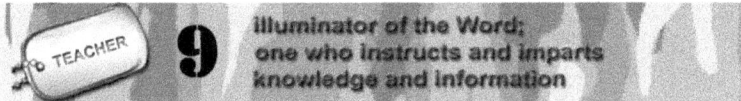

9 illuminator of the Word;
one who instructs and imparts
knowledge and information

TEACHER

THE TEACHER

Teacher: ("Toecan" – Old English) - Instructor, a giver of knowledge, a director, a discipliner

He has the Mind Of Christ to bring wisdom and understanding

(2 Peter 2:1) – *But there were false prophets also among the people, even as there will be false teachers among you.*

In my travel across the country over the last thirty years, I have seen a vast rising of people in the five-fold ministry. Never before have I met so many self-appointed teachers, evangelists, pastors, prophets and apostles.

When speaking with the members of the five-fold ministry, it was amazing to find out they were barely saved and did not have an in-depth knowledge of God's Word. Yet, they considered themselves to be members of the five-fold ministries, the governmental structure of the spiritual kingdom of God, which is responsible for the training of the body of Christ until they reach spiritual maturity.

(Ephesians 4:11-13) states, *And He gave some apostles, and some prophets, and some evangelists, and some pastors and teachers. 12) For the perfecting of the saints for the work of the ministry, for the edifying of the body of Christ: 13) Till we all come in the unity of faith, and the knowledge of the son of God, unto a perfect man, unto the measure of the stature of the fullness of Christ.*

The responsibility of the members of this government structure of God's kingdom is quite intense, as scripture warns us that we should not take to ourselves that which God has not appointed to us.

Remember to whom much is given much is expected. I once was invited as a guest speaker on television in Georgia.

When I was introduced to the host of the show, I was told that he was Elder so and so. The next time he stated he was Bishop so and so. Six months later he was Apostle Bishop Elder so and so, and yet he had not received any further education in God's Word.

Please do not get me wrong, I believe firmly in the five-fold ministry. I have met true Apostles, Prophets, Evangelists, Pastors and Teachers. They have blessed my life with the knowledge a wisdom that God had given to them.

My wife, Patricia, is a recognized prophetess of God, whom has not missed a prophecy given by her in thirty plus years. All of these people have paid a serious price for the position God has appointed to them.

We must remember what scripture states: *Strike the Shepherd and the sheep shall scatter* **(Matthew 26:31).**

Paul also warns that not many should seek to be teachers because of the great responsibility. Just as in the secular, teachers are instructors and are responsible for teaching students until they become knowledgeable in their chosen professions.

I know that when we are young, we do not appreciate school. We tend to see it as a prison, and the teachers are prison guards. It is only when we reach a level of maturity that we come to understand that the teacher is our friend, and they are there to help guide us through the maze of knowledge.

So it is in the kingdom of God. The teacher is given the responsibility of not only studying for himself or herself, but they study to obtain knowledge so that they can train others.

Even the great apostle Paul claimed that he was not self-taught but had the privilege of having a teacher. He told the Jews at Jerusalem that he was brought up at the feet of Gamaliel and taught in the perfect manner of the law **(Acts 22:3)**.

The Apostle Paul was thankful for the teachers that he had in his life and for the education he received from them.

I remember when my wife and I first came to the Lord. We searched everywhere we could for someone to teach us.

Although we spent hours in self study, there were things we still needed others to help us to understand. I cannot count how many times someone would come up to us and tell us we did not need any man to teach us because the Holy Spirit would teach us all things and bring all things to remembrance.

Yes, this is absolutely true, but it does not do away with the need of teachers to lead and guide us. What would happen to our children if all of a sudden they decided they didn't need to go to school anymore because the Holy Spirit would teach them all things?

Praise God for the Holy Spirit and the gifts of knowledge He gives to man, but we still must make an effort to go on to maturity and learn.

The teachers that God raises up for His divine purpose, and sends to instruct us, are gifted with knowledge not only of this world, but also of the wisdom that comes from above **(James 3:17)**.

It is the hope of any good teacher that he or she can instruct their pupil(s) so that they not only reach the level of knowledge that the teacher has obtained, but that there would come a day that the pupil would surpass the teacher.

Every parent is proud when their children accomplish more than what they have done. Many fathers and mothers work hard at manual jobs so that their child/children can go on to be more than they ever were. That is the same self-sacrificing attitude that a loyal teacher has concerning their students, especially those who put forth an honest effort to learn and succeed.

This is the way of the Spirit of God. He gives the same opportunity to all men to learn, but to those who make an honest effort to learn the things of the kingdom, He gives more to them. The more of ourselves we give to God, the more of His Spirit He gives to us.

Remember the word of John the Baptist, We decrease so that He may increase (**John 3:20**).Yes, the Spirit will teach us, but we must be willing to learn.

Many say that we need no man to teach us, but how shall we learn if there are no teachers? Jesus himself was called Rabbi, which means teacher. The disciples learned the things of God and His kingdom at his feet. In **(Acts 4:13)** it is recorded that the high priest and his followers took notice that Peter and John were unlearned and ignorant men, and they marveled at them, and took knowledge that they had been with Jesus.

Thank God for the wonderful gift of the office of the teacher.

It is through the love, patience and concern of these wonderful people that we obtain knowledge and maturity.

It is the responsibility of the teacher to clear away the confusion, and to bring to the light through academics, that which is concealed in darkness of ignorance.

It is amazing to think that Albert Einstein, who came up with the mathematical formula E=MC, that changed the whole scientific world, had to be taught at one time in his youth like everyone else that two plus two equals four.

The rewards of the teacher do not come so much from finances as it does from accomplishments. Can you imagine the joy of the elementary math teacher(s), who first taught basic mathematical formulas to Einstein, the day that this great scientist discovered the advance formula of $E=MC^2$? This humble servant may not have been the one who discovered this amazing math equation, but they were the ones who set Einstein on the path of knowledge to discover it.

If the secular teacher was done away with, civilization would collapse and be no more, and civilized man would revert to being a barbican once again, and so it is with the biblical teacher. If Satan could destroy the office of the teacher, man would be in spiritual darkness. Society would sink lower into darkness than ever with the loss f the biblical teacher.

It is the job of the teacher to stand against the darkness of the adversary.

The job of the teacher is not easy, for as scripture states; *they war not against flesh and blood, but against spiritual wickedness in high places* **(Ephesians 6:12)**. This is true whether a person is a secular teacher or a spiritual teacher.

These wicked spirits in high places have been assigned to hinder and to destroy the works of the teacher.

If you do not believe this to be true, then simply take a good look at our public schools, not only those in the big cities but in the small town schools as well. Armed security guards or police officers are stationed at the doors of the school. Our children have to pass through metal detectors, drugs are everywhere, children are giving birth to babies, and children are killing children.

In some places your child can be beaten or even killed for the shoes or jackets they are wearing. I remember going to school and sitting quietly at my desk while the teacher was getting ready to lead the class in the Morning Prayer and the pledge of allegiance to the flag. We were taught to honor God, country and family. We were taught to respect authority. There was no carrying of guns to school, or talking back to the teacher.

What has happened to our classrooms? How did we go from the schools of yesterday to the chaos of today? If the truth be told, we simply let there be wicked godless spirits operate through the likes of Madelyn Murray O'Hair, a sworn atheist to remove prayer from school and then allow people to complain that saluting the flag of our great country was offensive to them and their children. So it became against the law to honor our flag and the sacrifice that was made by freedom loving patriots to keep our flag flying high as a symbol of our freedom

Remember this, the cross is the symbol of Spiritual freedom and the American flag is the symbol of physical freedom and both are hated with a passion by these wicked spirits in high places.

Teachers, I would say to you: Know your enemies. It is not enough to have academic knowledge. You must also have spiritual knowledge in order to protect those who you are given charge over. Teachers, whether you believe in a spiritual kingdom or not you are in a war. These spirits hate you and what you stand for. You may not believe that a rattlesnake can harm you, but if he bites you, whether you believe it or not, you will get sick and die!

SPIRITUAL TEACHERS

Now I am speaking to the spiritual teachers about why it seems at times they are so unsuccessful. It is not anything that you have done wrong. In fact it is because you are doing something right, that this **opposition** has come against you.

The job of the teacher whether it is secular or spiritual has become quite difficult, simply because of the invasion of new age, liberal, and occultist thoughts and concepts. The influence of the Muslim and other religions, as well as the atheists, have all assaulted prayer in public places, along with teaching disrespect of our flag and what it truly stands for. May God's army of prayer warriors and intercessors unify and come together to stop these ungodly activities.

Teachers: please be aware that because of your position, you have come under the attention of spirits of wickedness which according to scripture dwell in high places. What are these high places you may ask? Well, they are both spiritual and physical.

If you believe in God: then you must also believe in the adversary who is known as the devil. As one person stated, the greatest trick the devil ever did, was to convince people he does not exist. In all reality, he does exist, and not only is he very real; he has a great army of fallen spirits as well as demons and other unclean spirits.

The army of the adversary is very organized.

Disciplined and in order in every city, village and town. There is a strongman placed over it! The strong man has a legion of spirits under his authority. They are given order to watch over everything in the strongman's area. They follow the command of their wicked spirit in high places, which stands in oppression of anything that is holy and pure. These spirits of wickedness have made it possible for the homosexuals and witches to produce lobbyist power in Washington D.C., to have the laws that they wanted, to be passed by the Congress men and women, and the senate that they put into position.

Their people backed by the wicked spirit in high places swayed even the race for the president.

Teachers the existence of these spirits can be found in the book of **(Daniel: Chapter 7)**, where he sees in a vision four great terrifying beasts. The first was like a lion with eagle wings. This was the symbol and strongman over Babylon, where King Nebuchadnezzar reigned. The next was like a bear that was unevenly made, indicating that one part of the country would be stronger than its other half. In the mouth of the bear was three ribs and it was commanded to devour much flesh. This was the kingdom of Medes and Persians who would over throw Babylon. The next was like a leopard having four wings and four heads. This was according to Alexander the Great who conquered the whole known world of his time. Shortly after Alexander died, his kingdom was divided among his four generals. Lastly, the final beast was so terrible and strong great iron teeth, it devoured and broke in pieces, and stomped the residue with its feet. It was diverse from the beast before it, and had ten horns.

Teachers, this is more than symbolism. It is the spirit world working through man to accomplish what it wants. These spirits or strongmen of wickedness are still working today to establish their kingdom of Earth. They will work through mankind to perform their desire and to accomplish the will of their dark master better known as the devil (or the adversary).

Teachers when you were given the position of an educator, that you now have, God knew what you would be facing and God trust that you were more than able to strand strong and overcome the adversities against you. Yes, the spirit of wickedness is strong and determined to have its way, to block the mind of man to keep him in the dark, in bondage as a slave to their master.

Yet, one greater than any strongman of evil, has over powered them through you, his chosen vessel of light, righteousness, and wisdom. Remember teachers, when you feel down and hopeless and overcome, all you need to do is call on the name of the greatest teacher that ever existed.

He knows all about the testing and trials you are going through. He knows that the tests are not sent to destroy you but to strengthen you.

Teachers; you know as an educator that as much as your chargers hate tests they are given not to hurt or shame your students, but to show them how far they have come and what they have accomplished. It is the same with us.

The tests are never to destroy, but they are there to reveal our weaknesses so they can by God's grace become our strengths. So, like when you promote a student who has passed all of their tests, **God will also promote you when you allow His tests to strengthen you.**

Yes, you have a strong adversary, but *greater is He that is in you than he that is in the world.* **(1 John 4:4)** May God strengthen you and empower you to as perform your office of a teacher.

Always keep in your mind that you are entrusted to shape and mold the minds of your students, until they come into the fullness of knowledge, wisdom and maturity.

Teacher; yours is a great responsibility. Turn to the author of all wisdom from above and seek his help. Who knows? You may be teaching and training another Samuel Clement (Mark Twain), or another Einstein, or a modern day Apostle Paul.

Teachers: *may the Lord bless you, may the Lord make His face shine upon you, and be gracious to you! May the Lord lift up His countenance on you and give you peace.* **(Numbers 6:22-27)**

10

TEACHER'S OPPOSITION
WICKED SPIRITS IN HIGH PLACES

10 stealer of the Word; delegates influences of control; high ranking, evil, supernatural powers; power of sin and evil in operation in this world

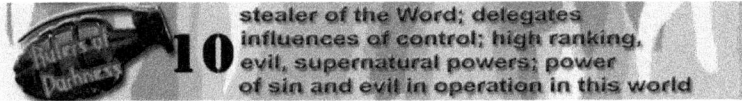

TEACHER'S OPPOSITION
Wicked Spirits In High Places

The Greek word for wickedness is *poneria*, which means depravity and particularly in the sense of malice and mischief, plot, sins and inequity.

Malice = 1: A desire to harm others or to see others suffer, extreme ill, will or spite.
       2: Law – The intent, without just cause or reason, to commit a wrongful act that will result in harm to another.

Since Satan is known as the prince and power of the air, these wicked spirits in high places are under his leadership and authority. These wicked spirits work malice and evil in the high places. They are responsible for spreading all kinds of filth. Their main purpose is to deceive, mislead, and destroy mankind.(**Philippians 2:23)** speaks on how these spirits work in the lives of unbelievers and attempts to bring believers back into bondages that they were set free from.

The great apostle Paul warns us that we were in a battle not against flesh and blood but against wicked spirits in high places.

I remember when I was once asked to speak on the growth of witchcraft in America today; I had shocked the interviewer when I told him that the *spiritual witch* was not as dangerous to society as the political witch was. He looked at me in complete amazement and asked what I meant by that statement. I explained to him that the *spiritual witch* was out to obtain power for themselves and their covens, and they were not interested in converting the whole world to their point of view.

They only wanted power for themselves and their followers. The opposite is true of the political witch.

They do not only want personal power and control, they want absolute power and control.

They're out to change the law of the land to be in their favor. They want to bring not only this country, but every nation in the world, under their authority and the authority of their leader.

In the beginning of this century, up until the sixties, witchcraft was done in secret. No one openly admitted that they were witches. Those who practiced the occult art took vows promising to keep everything a secret at the cost of their very lives if they revealed any of this mystical information to any outsider.

The term *"wicca"* did not exist. Every practitioner of the black arts was either a satanist or a witch. Things changed in the sixties when Gerald Gardener, with the help of Doreen Valentine, translated the works of Aleister Crowley's "The Golden Dawn" to a lesser satanic approach.

The new school of thought began to take place and the birth of Wicca began. The witch who had hidden in their craft for years under the threat of blood oaths taken, were now coming forward to admit openly that they were 'wiccan' and enlightened ones.

New schools appeared everywhere. These were the followers of Gardener, Alex Sander, traditional school, hereditary witches. New leaders appeared everywhere. Gardener and his wife, Alex Sander, The Frosts, Silver Ravenwolf, Scot Cunningham, and Lori Cabot, the official witch of Salem

whom was appointed by a former governor of
Massachusetts.

Laws were changed to protest the rights of witches, to give
them holidays, and to provide chaplains in the military for
them. Laws were passed in the favor of witches, new agers,
homosexuals and lesbians, making it a crime under the hate
law to speak openly against them and their practices. Laws
were changed to take away the rights of the Christians to
have Bible studies in school, to pray in public places.
Chaplains could not call on the name of Jesus when they
prayed.

Even the president stated that we were no longer a Christian
nation under the God of the Bible but were a nation of many
Gods and religions.

How did this happen? It happened because good men stood
idly by while evil men under the influence of wicked spirits
in high places changed the laws of our land in their own
favor. Not only were our laws changed but our educational
system, our medical system, even our entertainment was
changed. The minds of our young people are being altered
through violent video games.

It was once stated that if you could control the minds of the
young for one generation, you could eventually control the
entire world. Teachers, Satan is aware of this and has
unlimited resources with the finances as well. He will spare
no expense to obtain his goal.

He wants to be 'God' and to rule all of creation. He wants
for all men to worship him and to be in bondage to him. His
minions of wicked spirits will spread his perverted form of
knowledge everywhere.

He will replace truth with the lie. You as a teacher are the
only defense against the assault that is coming from satan's

kingdom. You teacher can stop the filth from being poured out on the minds of the young causing them to be filthy and perverted.

Programs like 'No One Left Behind' or "No Student Left Behind " have done more harm to the education of our children then good. Many of the students of today can barely read and do only basic math when they graduate from high school. We are not teaching them to be the best that they can be. We are just pushing them through. It is like the church that does not disciple the believer.

They are not being trained to be mature spiritually powerful followers of Christ. They are just being entertained. We are just scratching "itchy ears."

Teachers, remember satan does not care about how much you talk and entertain people. He just does not want you to instruct and empower them to get them to stand in the maturity and strength of the Spirit of God.

It is time to fill the mind of the young with the knowledge that is pure and holy which comes from the throne of God. **(James 1:7)** and **(James 4:17)**

It is time to push away the perverted knowledge and the vain philosophy of satan and sinful men. We need to instruct our young in the way(s) of the Lord and true wisdom. Remember that all it took to have our schools change forever was for the people of God to stand idly by. While on ungodly person took prayer out of school turning them more into a penal institution then an institution of learning

Teachers, you need a solid foundation in the Word of God, knowing right from wrong. You need to have an awesome support system that will be there for you through your church families and other believers in your communities to battle the fiery darts from the enemy camp.

Teachers, we must never stop studying. You must be an intense learner because you cannot teach what you yourself don't know. You are to impart the truth to your student and it is the Spirit of God that will help your student to get the discernment into the knowledge's usage.

What you learn of God's Word is to be of a transforming character. It is to help pupils be more obedient to the will and ways of God, so that they may do His will and therefore glorify God.

What a high privilege then to be engaged in teaching others God's precious Word! To be effective in His teaching, every Bible teacher and Christian education worker should be a student of God's Word, and should pray with the psalmist:

"Teach me thy way, O Lord" **(Psalms 27:11; 86:11)** and *"Teach me thy statutes"* **(Psalms 119:12,26, 64 68,124 and 135)**.

Teacher, *train up the child in the way he should go, and he will never depart from it.* **(Proverbs 22:6)**

APOSTLE — governmental church leaders; earthly head of church; builder; special messenger of Jesus to whom was delegated authority to do certain tasks and be His witness

PROPHET — eyes & ears for church; mouthpiece for God; communicated message of God to the people & communicated back to God the response or message from the people

EVANGELIST — mouthpiece for kingdom; calls to repentance; points to way of Christ; gatherer, breaks chains of bondage; opens eyes of spiritually blind; brings both physical & spiritual healing

PASTOR — assigned under-shepherd who feeds, guides, & protects flock from attacks of his sheep's enemies, he would give his life for the sheep in his care; teaches, leads & feeds flock

TEACHER — God's gift to us to teach truth of His Word & kingdom; illuminator of the Word; one who instructs & imparts knowledge, information & understanding; held accountable for teaching

The 5-Fold Ministry © 2014 H. A. Lewis Ministries

Satan	destroyer; great opposer or adversary of God and humankind; the personal name of the devil
Principalities	blockers of God's message; a powerful ruler, any type of rule other than the rule of God himself over a region
Spiritual Wickedness	collective organization of all of Satan's devilish spirits that work evil and mischief for the purpose of humanity's deception and destruction
Powers	ability or strength to perform an activity or deed; having power, but not authority; have physical strength as a lion, bear or wolf
Rulers of Darkness	stealer of the Word; delegates influences of control; high ranking, evil, supernatural powers; power of sin and evil in operation in this world

Opposition to the 5-Fold Ministry © 2014 H. A. Lewis Ministries

About the Author

Dr. Henry Lewis is the President of an Apostolic International ministry called Joshua International. Joshua International offers Biblical Leadership Training and Spiritual Over comers material. Henry Lewis is a Sicilian Jew and a descendent of Andrew Murray.

He is married to his wife, Patricia, for over 42 years. They have been in ministry since 1980 and have two children.

Dr. Lewis has authored 10 books. The first book called A Quest for Spiritual Power is now translated in Arabic and in French. The Arabic book was printed in Egypt and the French book was assembled and translated in Switzerland and printed in France.

Dr. Lewis is a sought-after speaker and author, teaching at churches and conferences along with numerous TV guest media outlets teaching on subjects such as: spiritual warfare, revival, transformation, revelation, transformational prayer. Henry evangelizes and teaches with international prophetic leaders in 10 countries.

His testimony of his former occult leadership experiences of seven generations has enabled him to share the love of God and his delivering power.

Charisma magazine shared is testimony in 2000. 750,000 Hindus translated the article in their language and accepted Christ.

Dr. Lewis attended several colleges which led to obtain three Doctorates in Counseling, Theology and Christian Education.

Henry and his wife have established churches in the US. Their first church was by the assistance of Aimee Semple McPherson's son, Rolf McPherson, who believed in their calling. Later, Dr. Roy Hicks, Sr. (friend who worked at Angelius Temple with Rolf McPhearson) supported them as well.

Henry and Patricia's spiritual foundation was formed from: Dr. Leonard Heroo (Apostle and President of Zion Bible Institute), McPherson), Evangelist Robert Schambach, Prophet David Wilkerson and Derek Prince, Lester Sumrall etc.

Henry's passionate thirst for the knowledge and truth of God's word led him to obtain a deep relational experience with his Lord and Savior, Jesus Christ – and not a religion – so he could hear and know the voice of God.

His vision is to teach and train a courageous generation the incorruptible Word of God and introduce the power of the Holy Spirit. Henry and Patricia's goal is to bring restoration to all nations including the Native Americans. His wife, Patricia is of the Iroquois nation.

Henry & Patricia coordinated large transformation events in New England under the 'Vision for New England" network which began in Salem, Ma with the help of Rev Ken Steigler & local pastors. Daystar programming promoted the events for 2 years. A transformation video was edited that shares the signs and wonders and miracles that occurred.

Dr. Henry Lewis is ordained with the Assemblies of God.
Henry is also ordained Rabbi through Asher Intrater from the Revive Israel Ministries

He is available for speaking.

Books

A Quest for Spiritual Power - Redeemed from the Curse - testimonial

Choisi Par Le Maitre: En quête de puissance spirituelle - French translation

A Quest for Spiritual Power - Arabic translation

Nimrod - How religions began and how it applies today

Spiritual Opposition to the Five Fold Ministry

The Secret Names of the Strongmen - study material & prayer manual

Jezebel - human or the spirit of baal?

The Dispensation of the Lion and the lamb

The Return of the Days of Noah

Available on Amazon

For More Information

In the US write:

H.A.Lewis
Joshua International

P.O. Box 1799
Maricopa, AZ 85139

Email: Info@halewis.org
Email: Info@ joshua-edu.org

To order or inquire of additional products, visit us online

Website: www.halewis.org
Visit us on face book

Book Cover Artist: Debbie Wheat
Contact: **izayu54@yahoo.com**

Book Co-coordinators

Grace Miller
Patricia Lewis